FORGIVING MURDER

THE VOICE
OF REASON

A TRUE STORY ABOUT
THE DEVASTATION OF
MOB VIOLENCE

ANITA LAMBERT

First Published in Canada Dec, 2016 by Voice of Reason

ISBN: 9780995854208

Book Cover Design: Greg Salisbury
Typeset: Greg Salisbury

I dedicate this book to my boy, Eric. It is my sincerest wish to honor you with my words. Not all of my words are pretty but they are all written with love in my heart: my love for you, my family, youth, and my human community. May my words be a blessing to others.

~Love – Neenee~

I would also like to also dedicate this book to the memory of Gail, Eric's mom. Sometimes a broken heart just can never be repaired. Rest in Peace!

Testimonials

Anita's personal connection to the tragic events that led to the death of her nephew resonates with my students. They come to an understanding about how drugs and alcohol significantly affect their ability to make good choices. My students also develop a deep respect for the number of people and the depth of impact that a teenagers death results in. Finally, the message of forgiveness is one that both astounds and inspires all those who hear it. Her message is worthy of deep reflection and infinite praise and I am grateful that she has been strong enough to share it with the world.

Alana Stelten-Routhier

Masters of Education in Leadership (M. Ed)

B. Ed (Secondary); B. Sc. (Math)

Anita courageously shares her heartbreaking personal tragedy to raise awareness about the senseless acts of violence our youth are facing. Her selfless perseverance and voice of reason are an inspiration. She defines her experience and chooses to not let it define her.

Marsie Tyson

Executive Director Rocky and District Victim Services Unit

Acknowledgements

I would like to acknowledge the support I have received from my family – both immediate and extended. My husband has been patient and encouraging with my writing and my commitment to sharing Eric's story, my children have given me ideas throughout my journey and have helped me develop aspects of my trade label, Voice-of-Reason. A special thank you to my brother, Grant, for not standing in the way of my dream. I know that this book will bring up memories and feelings that we would all like to leave rest. I would like to thank the teachers and caregivers that have invited me to speak with their students and charges. This has been valuable practice in telling my story.

I would like to acknowledge The Mountaineer Publishing Company (Rocky Mountain House, Alberta) and Stu Salkeld for allowing me to reprint the May 22, 2012 article that highlighted my attendance at the Communities Celebrating Life Symposium.

I would also like to say how I appreciated the discretion the media used when reporting Eric's death and ensuing trials. The news teams approached us politely and were respectful of my children and did not invade their space.

I would like to thank Jazmyn Vogt for allowing me to use photos that she beautifully doctored to reflect her love for Eric. Also, I would like to thank her mom, L.m Kozak for her beautiful words in "He Didn't Know". She wrote this poem right after Eric passed away. I don't think that Jazmyn and her mom know how much the angel picture and poem means to my entire family. We all have a picture made with the poem on it in our homes in remembrance of Eric.

Thank you to my writing coach and partner in publishing, Julie Salisbury. I would never have completed this manuscript without you guidance.

I would like to thank Eric's friends for loving him. He loved all of you so much. As you read this story you may feel singled out negatively by the words I have said. It is not my intention to hurt you. I have to tell my story on how I felt at the time all of this happened. I know that the actions of some was the overwhelming disparity they felt for such a devastating situation.

Thank you to everyone that assisted my family and myself during years of anguish. One positive that always shines through in a disaster is the human capacity to help those in need. The first Christmas without Eric, friends and people that really did not even know my family provided supper and Christmas baking. Thank you Brenda for taking my children when I needed to be at the hospital and for years after when I had to go to court and most especially for being with Clarence when he had to tell Matt that Eric passed away. Thank you to all my friends that brought food, helped with my children, prayed for my family, and assisted in any way they could. I will never forget the afternoon when my girlfriend, Tanya, came over and just massaged my back. She did not talk and she did not try to fill the silence, she just wanted to give me comfort. Thank you to Pastor Dale who helped me survive and was a wonderful support to me and my entire family.

I want to thank God. With God all things are possible. There is not a moment in this endeavour that He has not been with me and been my strength.

I would also like to address the defendants in Eric's death. It is my greatest hope that you have moved forward and made a change in your life. Do not let the past define you. You also have the choice to have an amazing life. Take accountability for your actions, work towards living a life of positivity, and never fall back into the realm of hatred again - Do right by your community, your friends, your family, and mostly importantly by yourself. Give up your addictions and take hold of your mind, body, and soul. As Ghandi so eloquently said: BE THE CHANGE YOU WANT TO SEE IN THE WORLD.

Contents

PROLOGUE

You could say I am just an ordinary gal. I have three children. Two are graduated now and the youngest is in grade nine. For the past twenty-one years my whole life has revolved around them. I have been on every sports board imaginable, read in every classroom from K-5, baked cookies, slathered sun screen on field trips, and road the cheese wagon too many times to count.

I now drive a cross over but yes, I use to have a minivan. I tend to get really excited when Tide goes on sale at the grocery store. (It is kind of a highlight to my week). I am most happy for those thirty seconds on Monday (that is clean house, laundry, and change bed day) when everything is perfectly put away in the drawers, the house is spotless, and the beds have crisp linens on them.

For excitement I walk my dog or go for a bike ride. Oh yes, I also have a bit of an addiction to cop shows and I am a voracious reader. I enjoy travelling with my family and camping to me is a luxury.

I don't cross fit, enter mud hero races, or ice climb. I'm

not versed in the New Age organic lifestyle. Nor am I up to date on the latest fashions. I wear whatever grabs me at the time. My home is not decorated around today's new fad. (I tried that once and discovered I prefer spaces that bring peace to me not show pieces).

You might say I am one of the most boring people you have ever met that is until you get me talking. Talking about one of the most out of the ordinary horrific darkest unimaginable experiences a person has ever had the disadvantage of living through - MURDER!

By the grace of God I have made it through into the light and have started living again. I have made it my mission to change a little piece of the world and encourage others to choose a path of light in their own lives - choose to not abuse drugs and alcohol, choose to stay safe, choose to control their own power in their lives, and to choose forgiveness over hatred. The last one, choosing forgiveness, is possibly the hardest one to attain.

It is my sincerest hope that as you read through my story that you gain the power to control your life, make good choices for yourself, and learn the healing power of forgiveness.

God Bless.

Anita

Forgiveness is agreeing to live with the consequences of another person's sin. (Neil T. Anderson)

CHAPTER 1
ERIC

When I was sixteen I had the pleasure of becoming an Auntie. I was an Auntie to not just one but two babies - twins. On April 30th, 1987 my nephew, Eric Olsen, and niece, Kristen Olsen, were born. It was a day that will stand out as one of my life blessings.

At sixteen I had the advantage of no responsibility or accountability on how I could spend my time, energy, or money on my darling nephew and niece. I got to play all day, spoil all day, and at the end of the day I would hand them back to their mom and dad to deal with the tedious tasks of parenting. I was in my element.

Since, I was so young when Eric and Kristen were born I bonded with them on a different level than a lot of Aunts do. They were more like younger siblings to me. I was definitely their cool Auntie growing up. They loved to spend time with me at my apartment, the park, their grandparents' house, and camping. I would do crafts, play on the slide and swings with them, watch movies, and buy them really noisy and annoying toys.

Even at birth, 8lbs7oz twin, Eric was always big. When Eric was a young child people would expect so much of him because they always thought he was older than he was due to his size. This tended to cause problems for Eric because he was impulsive and did not think things through and then add size to the situation he often found himself in trouble. The labels ADD and ADHD were just being introduced when Eric was younger and there was not a largely recognized understanding for children displaying the symptoms of these types of disorders. Children were thought to just be "bad". This created difficulties for Eric in his behaviour and acceptance among the general public.

I am not sure if it was my age or just who I am and how I identify with people that don't fit the norm, but I was always able to handle Eric better than most people could. If he was misbehaving I could get him to stop. While others would yell at him if he wasn't performing the way they thought he should be I knew that was pointless, he would just misbehave more. Yelling turned off any part of Eric that would have paid attention to what was being expected of him. If he was angry I could get him to see reason. I had a way of just talking to him that he would respond to. We shared a special bond.

Neenee and her babies, Eric and Kristen. June 1988

Eric and Kristen could never say my name right so I became Neenee. Eric was always Neenee's boy. As he got older we continued to share a very strong bond. And, to most people's confusion he continued to call me Neenee. He would introduce me to his adult friends even as Neenee.

Even as a small child Eric required more attention and guidance than his sister. He was always up to something or into something. Eric was a blonde haired, blue eyed looking little angel but underneath he was a little hellion.

Eric was always doing the extreme even at a young age. If there was a jump to hit with his dirt bike he was there, if there was a cliff to dive off of into a pool of water he was head first, and if there was a scrap to get into he was in the middle. Decision making and impulse control were not his strong suits.

Along with the extreme behaviours also came extreme care and love. Eric was fiercely protective of his twin sister and little brother. He could torment them all he wanted but no one else dare cause them upset or harm. He was generous, gentle with younger children, and loved his family beyond measure. If you were fortunate enough to be his friend you also received this unconditional love from him.

Even In Death He Was a Friend Held in High Regard!
Photo By: Jazmyn Vogt

As an adult Eric was one of those bigger than life people. You know the type - they fill every pore of a room as soon as they walk in the door. Eric not only commanded a personality the size of a small country he was also nearly six foot seven. He was a large man that many referred to as: The Giant. You would not find a more loyal friend, he was caring and attentive to those he loved. He was never shy to hug you in public or tell you he loved you. He possessed charisma, charm, and confidence. He lived and loved to the fullest.

Eric wore his emotions on his shirtsleeve for the world to see: if he loved he loved completely, if he hated he hated deeply. There was no simple middle ground for Eric, it was all or nothing. You did not want Eric to have an aversion to you.

Ultimately this character trait of all or nothing Eric displayed led to horrendous choices, bad friendships at times, and illegal behaviour. I would love to describe Eric as an outstanding positive goal driven citizen but that would not be true. He had amazing qualities but he also had a darker side. I believe I have to be completely transparent as I tell my story. I am writing this book to make a positive change in the world. Honesty is imperative to the fabric of my story. We must all be accountable for our own actions throughout our lifetime and take ownership of our own life story.

There is always a starting point that needs to be established when telling a story. It does not matter if it is a tale of fiction, a nonfiction book, or an account of circumstances leading up to a crime. In the justice system this staring point is called a statement of facts. Establishing a statement of facts is one of the most challenging facets of court procedure. The statement of facts leading up to Eric's death are dubious at best. The court is charged with establishing the statement of facts. The statement of facts is an agreement that opposing lawyers use as a setting for the pre-existing scenario of a crime. This statement of facts will not necessarily reflect the true circumstances, feelings, or actions between parties but it is used as a starting point for establishing a feel of the two opposite sides and to lay the stage, theme, and setting for the production of trial. I know without a doubt that both parties involved acted or choose to act in an irrational manner and a death ensued. For the purpose of my story I am going to lay the facts out straight up. I am not going to gloss them over or embellish them. I am just going to lay them out so you get a sense of the conflict and setting of scene. I am going to be truthful even though I would like to hide some of the facts.

It was said that Colin Bibaud, one of the men that killed Eric, and Eric had first clashed in 2006 when a drug deal went bad. Eric allegedly tried to run Colin off the road on the Yellowhead Highway. I saw with my own eyes the damage that Eric's car sustained from this road rage. I don't know for certain who did what to who first, but I do know that instead of just parting paths and letting each other go they kept their mutual dislike of one another fueled by despicable actions and words. Each one of them had to be the "man". You know what I mean - a punk assed guy who thinks he is all that and no one is going to get the better of him. The mutual hatred between Eric and Colin Bibaud created a division in their community and within their social structure. It was consuming and relentless. There was Eric's side and then there was the other side - make your choice.

I am embarrassed and appalled to have to say drugs were a motivating force in this hatred, both used and sold drugs. No one wants their loved one seen in this light. This is one of those facts that I would prefer not to share but it needs to be. The whole point of me telling my story is to influence positive choice in others. I must realize negative choices too so others can make better choices for themselves. It was my understanding from others who knew Eric that Eric and Colin did not have this onetime event. There were more occasions of discourse between the two of them. Without Eric alive I cannot substantiate these claims. Truly in the end it doesn't matter. Eric is still dead and so many lives have been altered by bad choices.

Eric's father and my brother, Grant, summed up the statement of facts better than anyone when he spoke to the media. He said, "Nobody was innocent in all this, my son included. There are other ways to resolve conflicts than what we saw here." Grant also told them that his son's death and the circumstances surrounding it were senseless.

CHAPTER 2
THE STAGE IS SET

Every story has a beginning, middle, and end. It has a plot and conflict, setting and theme. I will lay out all of this for you except the ending. I am going to take my lifetime to perfect that!

It would be fair to say Eric displayed a large level of cockiness as well as charisma and charm. At times he did not keep his cockiness under control. As much as I loved him I have to be brutality honest that decisions and choices he made escalated the events of his death. Unfortunately he paid the price for his actions with his life. He received an unjust death sentence. He wasn't given the normal sentence of being held accountable for his actions.

Eric had different sides. The sides he shared with his family was loving and kind. He was attentive and interacted with everyone in his family from his grandparents to his toddler cousin to his aunties and uncles to his adolescent cousins. Examples of Eric's character are: he would make time to come and sit with his terminally ill grandmother or he would play basketball with his little cousins or even watch baby cartoons with my youngest son. He was respectful and did not act inappropriate.

Eric And My Mom Shortly Before He Was Killed

Then there was Eric's other side: the one that sold illegal drugs, partied, took drugs, was known in his town for being a "bad" boy. He hung with a fast crowd and was not above getting himself into trouble with the law. This was the impulsive and rash decision making Eric.

When Eric turned twenty he started to change his outlook on life. He wanted to start settling down; have a steady job, a steady girlfriend, maybe buy his own place, and refrain from some of the extreme behaviours he had so carelessly engaged in up until then. He was turning into a responsible adult with goals and ideals.

The night of May 25, 2007 in a bar in Stony Plain, AB Eric decided to put an end to the aging feud. He extended the olive branch to Colin Bibaud in a positive show of faith and was told to shove it in an unmentionable spot. From that moment on all bets were off. Eric had been disrespected and there was no way he was going to take that sitting down. Unfortunately in the end the old Eric won out and for that he would lose his life. Eric then turned bout face and made negative choices. Some of the negative choices he made were contributing factors to the repugnant events that played out over the course of the next couple days. It was the beginning of the end.

The night of Friday May 25, 2007 was the night Eric made the deadliest choice of his life. His lust for vengeance overrode his common sense. Eric's nemesis had disrespected him in a bar full of people and he was going to pay for it. There was no rationale in the matter, Eric just wanted revenge.

Eric and his crew followed Bibaud and his crew to a bush party. They laid in wake until the bunch came to leave. As the group was leaving the party Eric and his boys jumped them. They dished out a severe beating which left the rival group hurting. War was declared and Eric was the country to conquer.

Technology is really a wonderful thing but sometimes it is detrimental, and on Saturday May 26, 2007 this was the case. Word got out about the beating. People were texting one another, fueling fires, and laying challenges. Madness was boiling up. Sides were being chosen, alliances formed, and plans devised. Now Eric was going to pay for his disrespect. Retribution was in the plans. The texts that were flying between the two opposing groups were adding fuel to an already raging inferno of anger. There were fights being set up between the two rival groups. According to court testimony there were two earlier occasions in the day when the two groups were to meet to settle the score.

Darwin Haydey, one of Eric's convicted assailants, said that twice he and ten other people tried to meet Eric for a fight that had been set up by cellphone. The first time, Eric drove up and taunted the group at a 7-Eleven store in Stony Plain, Alberta and then drove off. The next occasion ironically the two groups were supposed to meet in a Church parking lot in Stony Plain. Eric and his boys didn't show up. After an hour Haydey and the others left.

During Saturday afternoon Eric's rivals also sat

around drinking, smoking pot, and watching mixed martial arts fighting. I think this is a significant side bar piece of information: in the ensuing court proceedings it was deemed by the experts that the level of violence that was used on Eric was in direct relation to the amount of violence some of the perpetrators had witnessed under the influence earlier on in the day. Feelings of hatred, mixed with alcohol and drug abuse, and enhanced by visual stimulation created a recipe of disaster.

DRUGS + ALCOHOL + HATRED = VIOLENCE
DO THE MATH

Later in the evening at an acreage party just outside of Stony Plain, AB disaster cooked up. Eric would lose his life and many lives would be changed forever.

Imagine a party attended by more than one hundred teens and young adults out of town at night: Music is blaring, a bonfire lights up the night sky, alcohol is going down the hatch, drugs are being passed around, skirmishes are being started and stopped, tales are being told, romance is starting and ending, everywhere you turn there is chaos. Cody Trautman, one of Eric's convicted assailants, testified that the party was chaotic and crowded when he and the others arrived.

From this point on the events of Eric's death played out as a Hollywood movie. It is incomprehensible that real life is actually as barbaric as the night of May 26, 2007.

Eric's had a young friend that was bottled the night of May 26, 2007 and nearly lost his eye. Cody Trautman was charged with common assault and Danny Friedrick, another convicted in Eric's death, was charged with aggravated assault in the matter of this attack. They used the sharded edges on the neck of a beer bottle that had been broken off to cut at this young man's eye.

Eric's friend was panicked for his life and did not know what to do or which way to turn. Calling the police or ambulance service was not an option he felt he could explore, he was at a party where illegal behaviour was taking place. He called Eric instead to come and help him out. Eric rushed to the rescue and very soon knew that he was the one that needed the rescuing.

In the court proceedings it was stated that Eric and his friends brought a golf club and baseball bats. Some said that Colin Bidaud's group brought weapons as well. There was a ratchet used and a police baton used by the Bibaud's group as well. Both of these weapons were used and admitted to in court.

Bibaud and his group were cruising between houses

in Stony Plain and learned that Eric and his friends were at the party. The group arrived at the party and all Hell broke loose. I say Hell because Eric went through a living hell until he was unconscious and even beyond that. Eric took off in the dark of the night to a neighbouring acreage and climbed up on the roof to hide from his attackers. Sadly, there were sensor lights that illuminated where Eric was hiding and a crowd of madness surged towards him. Within this surge of madness were those with retribution on their minds, there were others following along to take in the action because they knew the whole story, and then there were others there just because everyone else was and they thought they should join in but had no idea who Eric was or what had transpired.

Men with weapons were hoisted up on the roof and weapons were being passed up as well. Weapons of every shape, size, and make: fence posts, golf clubs, baseball bats, ratchet set, police baton, rocks, and bottles were being hurled towards Eric. He was being cornered from every side and there was nowhere to go except down. Down below was a crowd of people whipped up into an uncontrollable frenzy. People that did not even know Eric or the saga of what had transpired were firing rocks and bottles at him, screaming at him, and lusting for violence.

Mob mentality is a scary phenomenon. People that

would not ordinarily act in an aggressive and destructive manner join in because everyone else is and they are under the influence of drugs, alcohol, and raging emotion. Good people turn bad under a cult like inducement is basically what happens in a mob mentality situation. Provincial Court Judge Larry Anderson spoke to this in Joel Machmer's, one of Eric's convicted assailants, sentencing. He said one of the aggravating factors in the case was the mob mentality. During sentencing for Colin Bibaud Court of Queen's Bench Judge Sterling Sanderman said, " It was aggravating that the May 27, 2007, killing was a planned undertaking by a group that wanted to even the score and which evolved into mob mentality and involved many people, some armed, attacking one man."

The lone occupant of the house had no idea that Eric was up on the roof being attacked. He was crouching in his hallway calling 911 because he thought the crazed group of young people were trying to break into his house and kill him. Rocks were shattering his window, his house was vibrating from the top with people on the roof, no wonder he thought he was being invaded. Sadly, when he testified at one trial he spoke of how he felt guilty for not going out and trying to save Eric. Who in their right mind would intentionally get into the middle of a deranged mob even if he knew what was going on? Yet, that poor man has to live with guilt because of others' actions.

Eric fought for his life. He used a golf club and started to flail it at his assailants. He did hit Joel Machmer with the golf club. Eric got a few licks in but he was over powered, outnumbered, and he was repeatedly being struck from every side by weapons and dodging rocks and bottles being hurled towards him. Joel Machmer used a metre-long log to hit Eric in the shoulder and head. Cody Trautman threw a log at Eric and swung a ratchet at him. Trautman also testified that some of the men that were beating Eric hit him six or seven times. Charles George – Maze struck Eric with a police baton. With one last blow from a two by four he crumpled to the rooftop unconscious and broken.

The irrational had happened a man had been beaten unconscious. You would think that rational might take over at this point but no just stupidity reigned. The crowd below that had been whipped into a frenzy chanted, "Kick him off, kick him off!" And, with the careless roll of Charles George – Maze's foot Eric was hurled head first into the crowd below. Cody Trautman said it was like a herd of cattle… and everyone started kicking him. He was then repeatedly pummeled by feet breaking him into pieces. Several witnesses testified they saw Bibaud kick Olsen while he was on the ground. Darwin Heydey admitted to throwing rocks at Eric from the ground and then kicking him twice once he was pushed off the roof.

Eric's friends pushed themselves among the madness to rescue their friend, sirens were sounding, people were screaming, and Eric was dying. At this point Trautman claimed at trial that he sobered up and realized just how horrific the situation was. He jumped from the roof and tried to free Eric. He pulled Eric's tongue from his mouth so he would stop choking on it. Finally Eric's friends managed to pull him from the herd of crazed animals and drag him to the safety of a vehicle, only after they themselves had been hit and abused trying to reach Eric. Safe is a relative term really in this instance because it didn't matter that Eric was dragged to safety he was still going to die!

CHAPTER 3
DEVASTATING DISCLOSURE

May 27, 2007 was a beautiful day. You may not remember it but I do. It will stick in my mind forever for being one of the nicest days and one of the most hideous days of my life.

It was unseasonably warm that day. I was out in the backyard of my home gardening, having a fire, and spending time with my family in the morning. My mom was there sharing it all with me. The fact that she was there really was incredible because my mom was dying of cancer. She was having a very good couple of days so she was able to spend them at my home with my family and I. To travel the hour it took to get to my house was not something she could normally endure anymore. My son and husband even managed to get her down to the back of my yard on the quad. She was sitting in a lawn chair discussing my garden with me as I worked. My sons, husband, and dad were busy on a project in the backyard as well and we had a bonfire going to keep the early spring chill off of my mom.

Shortly before lunch I had to head out to a Girl Guides campout where my daughter, Kaeleigh, had a celebration luncheon with her troupe and their families. I was just getting ready to eat when my cell went off. I decided to ignore it because I was busy with Kaeleigh and I didn't want anything interrupting my time with her. My cell kept persistently ringing though and I finally answered it. This was the call that changed the course of my life forever.

On the other end of the phone my sister was crying and telling me that our nephew, Eric, had been beaten and was in a coma at the University of Alberta hospital. I nearly collapsed with the devastating news. I was standing by a spruce tree next to a picnic table, I dropped my plate, and slid down the tree. I could not even comprehend what was being told to me. The spring chill turned into a numbing cold that I could feel spread throughout my body. I remember my girlfriend coming to me and helping me up. My daughter, Kaeleigh, was standing over me with a look of terror in her eyes. In that moment she found out the awful truth that her cousin, Eric, could die. No nine year old should have to live through that experience. There was an eerie stillness to the once jovial crowd as the news was passed along throughout the gathering. Suddenly everyone started moving and talking at once. People who I hardly knew were offering support and help immediately. It is true that tragedy brings goodness from others to the forefront. My keys were taken from me against my protests. I was arguing I could drive, but thankfully more adept minds than mine prevailed. I was in shock, disbelief, and was in no condition to drive. My girlfriend loaded Kaeleigh and I into a vehicle and drove us the twenty minutes home.

Upon arriving home I had to break the news of Eric's condition to my husband, Clarence, two sons, Matthew and Josh, my dad, Howard, and my dying mother, Millie. What words do you use to explain something so senseless? The words spilled out of my mouth sounding unreal. This really could not be happening.

In the time it took for me to relay the news of Eric I witnessed my mom take a drastic downturn. Her fragile state of reprieve from the effects of her cancer were broken as the news sunk in. It was too much for her already taxed system to take.

After a long debate with my dad we decided to head to Edmonton. My dad wanted to wait and hear an update to Eric's condition. I knew that the only update we would be getting would be death. We did not have time to wait. My poor father was just trying to make sense of a senseless situation that he could not control and really did not want to face. Finally, my dad and I packed up and left for Edmonton, Alberta. Edmonton is about a two and a half hour drive from my home in Rocky Mountain House, Alberta. We were headed to the University Hospital of Alberta in Edmonton. The drive there was one of the longest ones I have ever endured.

Once I arrived at the hospital I was instantly plunged into a hazy nightmare of despair, hatred, and anguish. There was sadness in every corner, fear permeated the room, and hate jumbled itself among all the feelings.

My big brother, Grant, was in the waiting room with Eric's twin sister, Kristen, and his younger brother, Steven. There was a crowd of Eric's buddies milling around, there was more family members, health care professionals, and RCMP. There was a cloak of darkness hanging over everyone.

I rushed to hug my niece and nephew, and then I went to my brother. I cannot even explain the despair I could see and feel coming from him. My brother is one of the strongest men I have ever known. He is both physically and mentally strong. He is tenacious at facing hurdles head on and is not intimidated by adversity. At the moment I went to him I could see he was weak in his soul and spirit. I was terrified. If Grant was this upset it was REALLY bad!

Grant tried to prepare me for what I was going to walk into when I went into the room with Eric. I know that Grant told me things like: brain pressure, quiet, no touching him, hemorrhaging, crucial 24 hours but nothing really registered. I felt almost out of body.

When I went into Eric's room in the Neuro ICU I felt physically ill with grief and shock. I felt the burning foul tasting bile rise to my throat. My stomach revolted at the sight before me. There was my boy hooked up to more machines than I could count - there was one monitoring his heart, one to administer medicine, one to clean the toxins out of his system, one to monitor his brain pressure and activity, and another to ring if Eric died. His head was bandaged, he was bruised and broken, and underneath his wounds he was death white.

I stayed with Eric for hours. I would sing and pray, talk and cry, but nothing worked. He just wouldn't open his eyes. Finally, I touched him. What did it matter he was dying before my eyes anyways? The only time Eric would register a response at all is when his twin sister, Kristen, would walk into the room. If she came in to be with him his blood pressure would rise.

Nighttime came and I needed to take my father to my sister's home to rest. I left Eric with a whisper of, "I love you," and a prayer that he would be in this life when I returned in the morning.

Monday morning I awoke from a fitfully chilling sleep. It was not a nightmare that had left me cold. It was reality.

I arrived at the hospital first thing. My boy was still alive. Eric had made the night. Miraculously he had lived through the first crucial twenty four hours after his injuries. Most patients die within in this time frame. I started to have hope.

I left Eric that evening to return home and get my affairs in order so I could come back and stay for a while. I needed to find child care, arrange for Matthew to go on his grade six camping trip, I had a medical appointment, and I needed some changes of clothes. My dad had to get home to my mom because she was failing. She had a stroke from the intensity of the news of her grandson. My plan was to return either Tuesday night or Wednesday morning. Even the best laid out plans can be thwarted in a blink of an eye or a blip of a monitor.

CHAPTER 4
THE BLIP

Tuesday morning I got everyone organized and where they needed to be. Matthew was packed up and off to grade six camp for four days. Kaeleigh was at school and Joshua was with my girlfriend, Brenda. I went to my appointment in the afternoon and came home to get some chores done, clothes washed and packed.

In this time I started to lay out plans. Eric had not only made the twenty four hour mark but he had surpassed it. He was going to make it!

Now, I wasn't stupid - I knew that he wasn't going to come out of this unscathed. He was going to need rehabilitation, time, and support. I could give him it all. My home is large with many rooms, it is has easy access to everything, a wheelchair can be used in it with no problem. I was a stay at home mom, so time was not an issue. As far as support went, Eric would have everyone behind him from his own immediate family, to my family, to his grandparents and aunts and uncles, and of course his friends. Together we could make his recovery happen.

It would take time to realize the depth of his recovery and if he would gain his mental capacity back. An injury to the brain with the scope of seriousness that Eric had would definitely create issues for the rest of his life. I was up for the challenge.

Again all it took was a phone call to crash down all my hopes and drench me in misery. My sister called to tell me I had to get to Edmonton. Eric had a stroke, his brain had hemorrhaged, and he was going to die!

I was in my bedroom when the call came in. The next thing I remember was my daughter standing over top of me in the hallway. I had passed out and she had found me there afterschool when Brenda had brought her and Joshua home. Sadly that is how she found out her cousin was going to die - unquestionably. At four years old Joshua did not comprehend all what was going on but he knew it was bad and that he wouldn't get to see his big cousin, Eric, anymore.

Brenda phoned my husband, Clarence, to come home right away. I remember sitting on my living room couch shaking. Shaking so hard my teeth were chattering and I was so cold. It was shock. Once Clarence got home I started to calm down and formulate a plan of what had to be done. Brenda had to leave for a prior commitment but she would be back by 8:00 pm to pick up Josh and Kaeleigh. They would be with her from that time on until Clarence and I returned home. I had to find interim childcare for a few hours. I finally was able to get a hold of a neighbour teen who could come. I had to instruct her to only answer the phone if it was family calling. I did not want her to have to deal with the media or people phoning to see what was happening. Matt was at school camp and I had to get a hold of the camp to keep him away from any type of news so he would not find out prematurely about his cousin. His teachers were kept abreast of the situation so that nobody let it slip in front of him. I had to send a call to Kaeleigh's teacher and advise him on the situation.

Finally, all the little details were looked after and Clarence and I could start our trip to Edmonton. This was a trip of finality. I would never get to see Eric alive again.

On the way to Edmonton Clarence and I were rerouted because of a fatal collision. This added precious time to our trip. I was in a state of panic that I would not make it there in time. Without a doubt that was the longest car ride I have ever taken and I have literally travelled by car throughout Canada and the USA. On this final trip seconds felt like minutes, minutes felt like hours, and hours felt like days.

It was about 7:30 pm on Tuesday, May 29, 2007, when I finally arrived at the Neuro ICU Unit at the University of Alberta Hospital. I had arrived not to say hello and greet my nephew but to give a terminal goodbye, not a see you soon goodbye.

CHAPTER 5
THE END DOES NOT COME
NEATLY

As I walked into the waiting room outside of Eric's unit I felt it hard to breathe. There was a smothering air of despair and hatred pressing down on me. It was as though madness was draping and engulfing everyone there.

I could hear - retribution, someone is going to pay, homicide, MURDER! I could smell anxious sweat. I could see utter disbelief, shock, mournful sorrow. I could taste the bile rising in my throat again. And, I could feel the shaking, limp hugs of those that were there to say goodbye to Eric. All around me my senses were being bombarded with pain. My own inner pain was leaving me breathless and shaky. My system was in overload.

Eric had been moved to a larger monitoring room where those that loved him could be more easily housed to stay with him until the end. I entered that room with trepidation. Once I saw him I knew that I would no longer be able to hold on to my thought - this is a dream, it would be reality.

That room became my life for the next two days. I would not leave it unless the nurses needed to work on Eric or I was forced to take a break, or if one of my nephews or niece needed me. I remember getting angry at my husband and brother because they made me leave to go get something to eat. I think I was irrationally thinking that if I stayed the inevitable may not come. My place was at Eric's side. Clarence stayed with me throughout most of the ordeal. My family members would be in and out throughout the next two days trying to come to terms with what was happening. I was the one constant in the room. I was not leaving!

The room was a buzz with friends coming to say goodbye. Remember when I said my brother was one of the strongest men I have ever met? When Eric was dying he allowed all of Eric's friends to come in and pay their last respects. I know that I would not have been that generous if it was me. I would have wanted him all to myself, but Grant knew how important Eric's friends were to him and how important he was to them. I found some of them to be extremely intrusive. There was one time in particular four of his friends came in and one of the girls started lifting Eric's bedsheet to look at his body of bruises. I was appalled that she would cross the line of respect. It did not matter that he was in a coma. His body was his own and she should have respected that. She was not very happy when I asked her to put the sheet down and not to lift it again. I was not even rude about it. Which at that point in my life with the stress and exhaustion was amazing. It was the total disregard for manners from some of Eric's friends that added a mountain of stress to the situation for me. Eric's family was in and out of the room also. Family was different. They should have been there mourning him, saying good bye, and cherishing their last physical contacts with him.

There were periods of time when I could sit in quiet solitude with Eric. I would talk to him, sing to him, pray for him, and lecture him with boiling anger. Does that sound weird? Well I was mad and he was going to hear about it. Stupid moves on his part played a part in his death, therefore it played a part in my suffering. I would play the game, what if, over and over in my head. What if he would never have gone to the bar on Friday night? What if he would never have went and got his friend? What if he would have cleaned up his act and been more responsible? I hate the "what if" game! You never win!

One of the times I was completely alone with Eric

he sat up in bed. In the ten seconds that it took for him to lay back down I felt the most ecstatic feeling of happiness. He was coming out of the coma. The doctors were wrong. I called the nurse in right away. She gently shattered my dreams of hope again. Apparently an involuntary cough can cause a comatose, brain dead patient to rise, sit up, and fall back down. It was muscle response, not neurological response.

There was a rare quiet time on Wednesday afternoon when just Eric and I were alone together in his room. I was reading the newspaper to him. I am not sure why I thought I should do this but I was. There were stories of mayhem all over in the newspaper and it was very depressing. It really hit me at that point that I had to do something about all the negativity that was seeping into the culture and community around me. I promised Eric that his death would not be in vain. I told him that I was going to use his situation to help others. At the time I had no idea what that would look like, what it would entail, or how and when I would start. I made a covenant with Eric that I was not going to break and his death was going to mean something!

Every moment spent with Eric I was constantly watching his brain pressure monitor. One of Eric's doctors had explained to me what would happen when the true end became near. Eric's monitor would start reaching inordinate pressures and basically his brain would explode and sever his brain stem. I would be able to see the top of his head lift up like a cone with the pressure, explode, and then fall. A shockingly grandiose ending to a life taken.

CHAPTER 6
TIME TAKES ITS TOLL

As day turned to night and day again and night again the outside pressures surrounding Eric increased. The fuel of rage that was within many of the young people waiting for the end of their close friend's life was ready to ignite into an inferno of passionate hatred and retribution.

In their pain and grief a number of these young people turned to drugs and alcohol to relieve their pain. Ironic isn't it? Some of the mitigating reasons we were in this senseless nightmare was because of these substances.

Well we all know what happens when drugs and alcohol are consumed and emotions are running high - disaster. Surrounding Eric was the potential for disaster of extreme proportions. There was talk of retribution and killing those that took part in Eric's death. Eric was dying because of the beating he took so those responsible needed a beating. They deserved what was going to happen to them if his friends got a hold of them. That was the consensus among the young people.

In the center of this madness was my brother, Grant. He was constantly telling Eric's friends that Eric would not want them to place themselves in harm's way. My brother exposed himself to the media and begged for no retribution against those responsible. He was a stronger person than I was at that time. At that point in my life I would have been happy perhaps even ecstatic to hear that one of those evil creatures had paid the price for his actions. Grant would reiterate the need for control and no retribution for a long time even after Eric passed away. In one television appearance Grant said, "This event has been very devastating to Eric's family and to his friends. He's gone…he's not coming back. It is my expectation that anybody who considered Eric a friend that they respect his wishes and not get involved in any kind of retaliation or upsetting behaviour that would dishonour his memory."

Eric's Dad and my brother, Grant, Pleading for
No Retribution!

Even with the feelings of retribution that I had burning inside of me I also would dissuade Eric's friends from taking action. I did not want anything happening to them and I did not want another family experiencing the pain that mine was going through. I had to honor my brother's wishes as well and he had made it clear to everyone he did not want any retaliation.

You may have noted that I have not mentioned Eric's mom throughout this affair. His mom, Gail, was very much part of his life and our family. She just could not bring herself to be where her baby was going to die. Who could blame her? Losing a child is one of life's brutalist realities. Because of this my sister, Anneli, would stay with Gail until the end to support and comfort her. My sister was also very strong and could be a strength to Gail. Grant would go back and forth between the hospital and home to comfort his wife as well.

The last time Grant left the hospital he left me in charge of Eric. Whatever had to be done for Eric was up to me. I closed all visitation to Eric at this point except to family. Many people would still continue to push to come in. It was exhausting. I had to tell the nursing staff to not even come and ask me anymore. The answer was no!

I don't mean to minimize others' pain but there is

a fascination with devastation that can take over too. Some people just want to ride the drama train, there were definitely those at Eric's bedside that were his people but there were others that were acquaintances that wanted to play a part in the drama unfolding before them. Others, especially if they had never dealt with grief, didn't know how to properly behave. Being boisterous, obnoxious to the staff, riding wheelchairs down the hallways, and overall being disrespectful is not needed in a time of grief. Security would come to me and tell me how a certain person was behaving and that they needed to leave. This was not my problem to deal with. I stopped worrying about what was happening in the waiting room and simply kept my focus on Eric. When my brother had been in the hospital he was able to keep a better handle on everyone. This was selfish on their parts. My brother should have only had to worry about his family, instead he tried to look after everyone.

This may also sound callous but I was embarrassed by the way some of the people were acting. The nurses had had enough of the constant in and out and noise. There were other patients on the unit with grieving families that did not need the disturbance. I actually apologized to the staff and made sure they knew how upset I was by some of the behaviour. I did not want to be painted with the same alcohol and drug brush as some of those around. Call it pride, call it over sensitivity, I really don't care, it was important to me that the staff realized we were a family and we did not condone this behaviour.

My husband, Clarence, and I were alone with Eric when he imminently started to die. This was just shortly after my brother had left the hospital. Eric's monitor started reading deadly pressures. I called a nurse in and was advised to get everyone back immediately. I had to phone my brother and tell him to get to the hospital - NOW!

When I got a hold of Grant he told me, "Don't let him die until I get there!" What was I to do to prolong the inevitable? For the next twenty minutes I begged and pleaded with Eric to hold on until his daddy got there. Clarence went and woke up my nephews, found my niece and Eric's girlfriend, the rest of my family was notified and blessedly everyone made it in time for what we thought were Eric's final moments. He died "the first time" at approximately at 10:30 pm on Wednesday May 30, 2007.

One organ donor can save potentially eight lives and provide eyesight, skin, and other tissue to many others because of this Grant had made the decision to donate Eric's organs for transplant. Eric had to be kept clinically alive until his organs could be harvested. This means Eric was hooked up to life support. Eric did not die during a normal 9:00 am – 5:00 pm work day, because of the timing there was no transplant team at the hospital. The administration would not pay to have a team brought in on overtime. The nurses on the unit were devastated by this and they found people that would come in without pay to operate. Unfortunately Eric had to have a special x-ray taken with a radioactive dye. There was no dye at the hospital but there was some at a hospital across the city. No-one in the capacity to request this dye would arrange for the dye to be transferred to the hospital Eric was at. Grant was asked to wait until the following morning between 9:00 am and 10:00 am to finally detach Eric from life support. Please remember that my brother had been at the hospital basically since the early hours of Sunday morning, the rest of us had been to the hospital on off since Sunday as well, and some of us had not left in over thirty six hours it was now the final hours of Wednesday. In the early morning hours of Thursday my brother made the decision that as a family we could not take the stress any longer. He was going to unplug Eric. It took a bit of time to roundup the family once again. As we were all gathering around Eric's bedside to say our final goodbyes his girlfriend coded. Her heart had stopped and she was not breathing. Chaos erupted! A nurse called in a code blue team. We were all cleared out of the room. She was revived, taken out, my brother had to call her parents, and she was taken to ICU. Finally at about 1:00 am on Thursday May 31, 2007 my brother had Eric unplugged from life support. Eric was gone and a wake of destruction was left.

Picture By: Jazymn Vogt

Now Clarence and I were charged with the duty to go tell my mom and dad that it was over and their grandson was gone forever. What a tragedy! Never should a parent outlive their child, let alone a grandparent. It is not the natural order of life.

We then had to head to our home to tell our children that their cousin was gone. Once we arrived we told Kaeleigh and Josh. Josh was little and did not fully comprehend the idea of death. He just cried and cried because that's what everyone else was doing and also because he was so frightened of the unknown. Kaeleigh was nine years old and she sadly understood the consequences of Eric's death and all the gruesome details. Clarence headed to camp with my girlfriend, Brenda. The camp had been alerted to Eric's death and they had prepared a quiet place for Clarence to tell Matthew about Eric. What should have been a night of jubilation was a night of sorrow.

That evening Clarence left to head to camp I was in such complete despair. I could not eat, look after Josh, or function. I just sat on the couch and cried. My little Kaeleigh got her brother ready for bed and tucked him in with a storybook and prayers. She then helped me into bed and laid with me wiping my brow with a cold cloth. I am not sure if it was shock, overload, or just exhaustion but I was overheating. She looked after me until her daddy got home. What a trooper she was!

Eric Mitchel Olsen

He Didn't Know

He didn't say good-bye
He didn't know that he was leaving
He didn't have a clue
That today family would be grieving.

He didn't know about their tears,
So many lives filled with pain.
He didn't know that they'd be praying
To be with him again.

He didn't know there would be questions,
Yet no answers fill their hearts,
He didn't know that his family
Would be feeling torn apart.

He knows now as he crosses,
Into heaven above,
He sees and feels their pain
And send to them his love.

He is the whisper in the wind
As it strokes against their face.
He is the ripple in the water,
For he now lives in Mother Nature's
grace.

Picture By: Jazmyn Vogt
Poem By: L.m Kozak

CHAPTER 7
LAID TO REST

When someone dies at the hand of another an autopsy must be performed. Evidence is gathered, investigated, and filed away for the eventual court proceedings. Eric's body was not released to my brother for his funeral right away. It takes time for the Medical Examiner to finish all the detailed work that goes into an autopsy.

Eric was memorialized on June 10, 2007. There was a service at the local funeral home in Stony Plain, Alberta where he had lived. When my family and I left my mom and dad's house to attend the service an hour away my mom was in such bad physical condition that I pleaded with her not to die before we got home. My mom had to stay with a treasured friend because she was too weak to attend her grandson's funeral. It was compounded pain on top of pain. I was reeling from the emotions that were breaking my heart.

During Eric's service a reporter posing as a mourner

observed the service. After the service the funeral director and his staff had the guests make a human shield around Eric's family so our grief was not recorded on the six o'clock news. There were reporters and cameramen directly outside of the funeral home and also across the street, as well as hiding in the bushes. They wanted to catch a shot of the grieving family so their report could be sensationalized for everyone to see. I found this to be obtrusive and rude. Grief should not be a story of entertainment. It is a very personal emotion that deserves the respect of privacy.

It was my honor to write the Eulogy for Eric's service. It bothered me that when the reporter that snuck in to Eric's service presented their story in the newspaper they reported the wrong facts. It was stated that my brother had wrote the Eulogy. The reporter also recounted that there was only about one hundred fifty people in attendance for Eric's funeral. This was at least half of the actual amount of attendees.

Eric's eulogy was the hardest piece of writing I had ever done. Eight months later when I wrote my Mom's eulogy as painful as it was it still did not rip me raw like Eric's. In one thousand words I had to sum up my charismatic and vital nephew. This was my testament to the boy I loved and through my words I wanted to honor him and his family.

Eric's eulogy was read by two of his best friends.

(Your own lead in explaining that you have been asked to read the eulogy written by Eric's Auntie Neenee)

Crash, bam, boom, blast racing down the garden path. Scraped knees, upside down in trees, energy abound, with feet hardly touching the ground. Blond hair, cheeky grin, twinkling eyes, and a body that has always been oversize. I am sure all of you now have a visual of Eric in your head.

Eric Mitchell Olsen put the world into orbit on April 30, 1987. He was born a go-getter. Heaven forbid his sister made it out first. Because of timing and sheer determination he would be the older brother.

From day one Eric was a bundle of energy. Which might be noted –left those around him with lack of it, for always chasing after him. He loved to be outdoors – biking, fishing, swimming, boating, skiing and camping. Taking Eric to a pool or the lake was always interesting. The fish could take a few lessons from him. If ever you could soup up a tricycle I am sure Eric could find a way. He had a mean arm in baseball and loved to race up and down the soccer field. Eric was very loyal. As young children do they fight with their siblings once and awhile, well Eric and Kristen were no exception. Later on when Stevie got old enough to be annoying he and Eric fought too. BUT, God help anyone who thought they might give Eric's sister and brother a hard time. They had to come through him first. As a small child Eric always had a twinkle in his eye and a hug ready for you. This never changed as a grown man he never left a family function without a hug and an "I Love You". This could always be followed with a quick shove into his arm pit because he was so much bigger than everyone else.

The Bible says "Whatever you do, work at it with all your heart"

Eric lived this verse in completion. Everything he did in life was to the extreme with all his heart. It wasn't good enough for Eric just to ride his skateboard. He had to study Tony Hawk and become his rival. Snowboards were not to be ridden they were to be mastered. When Eric played baseball he was the best at what he did. Eric could throw a fastball at 88 miles per hour. An exceptional fastball from a normal sixteen year old would be between 60 and 65 miles per hour. No one could say Eric was normal. He loved to dirt bike. Cut lines and trails were for the faint of heart. Eric loved to fly and float. How you ask? Find yourself a borrow pit along the river like Eric did and see just how much juice you have in you. On one particular occasion Eric was sailing 50 to 60 feet across the river to the opposite bank having a blast. It was time to go so one of his friends shut off the fuel line on Eric's bike to pack it up. Unknown to Eric, who always had get the last ride in, he took off for one more jump and ended up landing himself up to his chest in water. What an extreme ride. After drying out his bike and replacing the oil Eric's worry of wrecking his bike disappeared. He was left with one incredible tale to tell. And, we all know how much Eric loved to tell a tale. Eric lived fuller in his twenty years than some do for an entire lifetime. What a reassurance to know that.

Eric and his buddies liked to have a lot of fun. Sometimes their idea of fun was a little off the wall. One time Eric's buddy, Kyle Eaves, decided it would be fun to rig up flashing red and blue lights on his vehicle and freak out their friends. One evening between Stony Plain and Spruce Grove Eric and Kyle were cruising and some driver on the road ticked them off. Well they decided perhaps he needed to be pulled over. On went the lights, and they proceeded to stop the culprit. What a shock to the system when they found out they just happened to pull over an off duty police officer. Not good. Unfortunately the boys got busted right behind Kyle's house. To add insult to injury the police could not figure out how to turn off the flashing light on Kyle's car. Typical Eric leaned over with that forever twinkle in his eyes and suggested they ask Constable Eaves. Not really the right thing to say but, worth the laugh.

Eric had three philosophies in life to live by:

1. *Enjoy Life to the Fullest*
2. *Take Care of Your Friends*
3. *Always Make an Impression*

I would say that Eric excelled in all three. He was passionate about his friends. If ever in need Eric would be there indeed. He was a wonderful son, grandson, nephew, and cousin. Eric always had patience for little people. If a small child was in a room you can be sure they would be on Eric's shoulders before too much time had passed. He was even known to lie down and watch a rousing show of Franklin the Turtle if his little cousins thought it was a good idea. He was never shy to express himself. Self-expression is what he was all about.

Today is a testimony of how many friends Eric had. Look around you; friends and family have come together from all places and walks of life. We have neighbors from next door, friends from Ontario, loved ones from out of town, and some from just across town. All of you are a testimony of friendship and love that Eric lived his life by.

If everyone had as many friends as Eric did the world would be populated with friends. What a wonderful place it would be.

As I left Eric's service I walked through a channel of young men dressed in white tuxes to honor Eric.

All the guests left through this beautiful gateway. As I proceeded through they started to wrap their arms around me and collapse on me. The raw pain that each one felt I could feel flooding off of them. It was a river of sorrow to my heart and mixed with my own agony it left me near comatose.

Throughout the luncheon that followed the service I dare say I was barely coherent. I did not want to be there, I did not want to speak to anyone, and I did not want one more person to hug me. I wanted to be left alone. I know that this sounds extremely selfish and immature. I also realize that I must have offended some people. I make no excuses for my behaviour. I truly was at my emotional breaking point and I could not handle interaction. There was nothing left in me to give.

My family was very good about protecting me. They recognized that I was holding on by a thread. They allowed only those closest to me approach and made appropriate apologizes to those that they turned away. I am sure that I seemed out of my mind to those that observed my behaviour.

After the luncheon my husband, daughter, and I went back to my brother and sister – in law's home to unwind. My oldest son and dad went back to Drayton Valley with friends. My dad did not want to be gone any longer from my mom. This was understandable considering the circumstances. During the time with Grant and Gail I found that I could talk and relive stories of Eric without being oppressed trying to deal with a crowd. It was during dusk sitting on the deck of his family home that I memorialized Eric.

CHAPTER 8
UNJUST REALITY

It took four years to see justice served to all the men that participated in killing Eric. In that time I spent countless hours in the courthouse in Stony Plain, Alberta and also in Edmonton, Alberta. This was time away from my family and sometimes with my family in tow, either scenario it was hard on them.

I would attend as many sessions of court that I could. In that time I would hear the details of Eric's beating retold time and time again. Imagine what it is like to relive the telling of the savage beating of a loved one. It created nightmares that I would have to live through for days after court proceedings. I was continually being traumatized by the mental pictures that would fill my mind - blood, chaos, terror, and death. It would take on a physical manifestation over time.

In the courtroom there was a constant media presence. Every action I made as a victim was being watched and recorded. There were no private moments until I would finally manage to get away for lunch or leave at the end of the day. Going to the bathroom even held its own hurdles. I could be washing my hands next to one of the killer's mothers, sisters, grandmothers, or girlfriends. Some of these women would send me petulant stares. I would want to walk over and smack that look right off their faces. How dare they? I was suffering because of the actions of one of their loved ones. Just being involved with one of those men made them guilty in my eyes.

The weapons that were used to kill Eric were in presence in the courtroom at the front. I would just look up and see them at the front of the room. There was blood and hair on some of them that was visible. It was gross and disturbing. I have watched my share of television and movies and I could imagine down to the last detail the horror of what Eric experienced. To be afraid for your life and to have to fight for it would be the ultimate helplessness.

There were a few disgusting moments in court that I cannot seem to put to rest. When I go into schools and present my story to youth these are a couple of the stories that disturb the students over and above the actual beating the most also.

One of Eric's assailants found it necessary to

throw me a wink or slight kiss blown in the air at any opportunity that arose when no one else was watching. He also would try and hold my stare throughout the proceedings. It was a form of intimidation that I would not let him win. At times I wanted to run up front and punch the bugger in the face but I always maintained my control and did not play into his hands. It would only make me look bad and stoop to his level.

Another time that sticks out in my mind is when one of the defense attorneys played underhanded by trying to provoke a reaction from my family right before sentencing, I assumed it was a ploy to try to get leniency for his client. He held up the murder book with a large picture of Eric in it facing the gallery. This picture was a complete nude of Eric on an autopsy table during the procedure. No one should have to see their loved one exposed like that. In death Eric was being humiliated once again. It was inconceivable to me to think that someone could be so cruel.

I wanted the men that killed Eric to suffer. I would think about it all the time. I would think about ways that they could be hurt to pay for what they did to him. I would hope that they would be used as someone`s boy toy in prison, or that they would be killed. I did not want them to just continue on in life as if nothing happened.

They stole my Eric from me and they deserved to pay.

When court was finally finished I felt so letdown by the legal system. I was reeling from the fact that the men that had caused such anguish in my family really did not have to pay a very big price for their actions.

The original charges that were laid against eight men in the death of Eric were:

Danny Michael Friedrick, then eighteen, Charles Montana George – Maze, then eighteen, Colin Peter Bibaud, then nineteen, Joel Luke Machmer, then nineteen, Darwin Murray Haydey, then nineteen, and Cody Trautman, then twenty one, were charged with second degree murder. Daniel Robin Furey, then twenty three, and Tristan Anthony Beyer, then nineteen, were charged with aggravated assault. Cody Trautman and Danny Friedrick were also charged with assault in relation to Eric's friend. These charges were upgraded to first degree murder and unlawful confinement for Charles George Maze, Colin Bibaud, Joel Machmer, Darwin Haydey, Daniel Furey, and Danny Friedrick. In the end none of the men plead or were charged with first degree murder or unlawful confinement.

I had no experience with the criminal justice system up until this point in my life. I did not realize that people charged with murder could be eligible for bail and let out. It made me sick how these men could leave jail and be living their lives in their neighborhoods like nothing happened while they had outstanding murder charges against them. How do you feel about the possibility of buying groceries or going to the gas station and having a murderer standing next to you? The conditions for their release were:

a. They had to each post a ten thousand dollar no-cash deposit
b. They had to keep the peace
c. They could not apply for a passport and they must remain in Alberta
d. They were prohibited from possessing any firearms, explosives, or controlled substances
e. They were not to have contact with each other, other than for employment purposes
f. They could not contact upwards of a dozen persons from the party who may later be called as witnesses
g. They had to abide by a curfew of 9:00 pm – 5:00 am
h. They had to refrain from the use of alcohol
i. They were not allowed to enter any licensed premises or attend any house parties or bush parties

j. They had to report to the Stony Plain RCMP detachment every Friday by phone during business hours

k. They had to provide, on the demand of a police officer, a blood or urine sample

On the day some of the men that killed Eric were released on bail the media played their release over and over on television. It captured pictures of them fist pumping the air and saying thing like, "In your face!" sticking out their tongues, and generally being obnoxious. They acted like they were the innocent bystanders and justice was served by letting them out. My daughter had surgery the day they were released. I remember seeing their release in the waiting room while waiting for her to be out of surgery. I crumpled into myself I couldn't believe they were out walking around and being so cocky and arrogant as they were leaving jail. Again my brother, Grant, took the high road. When he was contacted by the media for his response to the mens' release he told them he was disappointed but we had to let the justice system work.

Bail Release

By the time I got home from the hospital that night with Kaeleigh and my husband, Clarence, my two boys had seen the news of the killers' release. This release spurred a year and a half of multiple night terrors from my youngest son, Joshua. Joshua would awake in the night screaming in fright. He was scared the bad boys that took Eric away from him would come and kill him too. He would have to sleep with either his dad and I, sister, or brother to feel safe.

Some of the men responsible for Eric's death were not released immediately before their trials because they had broken conditions to other outstanding sentences against them and were incarcerated because of it. This spoke to the type of character they possessed.

In the Canadian justice system if an individual pleads guilty they are allowed the privilege of pleading to a lesser charge. It takes less court time and money to simply sentence an individual so the justice system looks favorably to a guilty plea and rewards the individuals accordingly, or at least accordingly in the eyes of the court. Several of the men that beat Eric choose this route to avoid a trial and possible stronger conviction.

Seven out of eight of the men charged in Eric's murder plead guilty to lesser charges of aggravated assault or manslaughter, Colin Bibaud was not one of them.

Danny Friedrick plead guilty to assault and received one year conditional sentencing. Conditional sentencing was basically the same as bail conditions. Daniel Furey, Tristan Beyers, Darwin Haydey, and Cody Trautman plead guilty to aggravated assault and received two years conditional sentencing.

Charles George-Maze received five years after pleading guilty to manslaughter. He received the largest sentence out of all the accused for his part in Eric's death. George-Maze beat him with a police baton after he was knocked down on the roof unconscious and then he pushed him carelessly with his foot off the roof. Eric crashed to the ground landing on his head where he was then pummeled by the surrounding mob.

Throughout Colin Bibaud's trial Cody Trautman provided key testimony for the prosecution. He would never waver on his story even when Bibaud's lawyer would try to undermine him. Trautman whipped a log at Eric and also swung a ratchet at him. Trautman spoke of how he thought the beating was over when Eric fell unconscious to the roof after being hit by Joel Machmer flailing a log. He jumped down off the roof once Eric was rolled off and tried to push people away from him. He also took Eric's tongue out of his mouth so he wouldn't choke on it. He told the court how Bibaud kicked Eric when he was down. Bibaud's lawyer tried to convince Trautman that he mistakenly seen Colin Bibaud but Cody Trautman would not falter on this point.

Colin Bibaud was sentenced to three years in prison for manslaughter on June 29th, 2010 after a long drawn out trial. The crown prosecutor could not prove first degree murder and unlawful confinement as originally charged. The court heard from an undercover police officer how Bibaud confided to him in jail that he beat Eric. He also told the officer that the fight had been prearranged. Bibaud during sentencing told the court how he had changed in the past three years and how he was on top of his addictions. It was very frustrating listening to him plead that he would be better off not in jail. Eric would be better off not DEAD and so would the rest of Eric's family.

The last accused to be sentenced was Joel Machmer. Joel Machmer also provided key details in Eric's assault. Joel beat Eric with a log on the shoulder and delivered the blow that laid Eric unconscious on the roof. Machmer showed his remorse by initially turning himself into the authorities. Machmer received two years in jail during sentencing.

Some of the witnesses throughout the court proceedings were hostile or non-believable. I would dare to say that they were compelled to be there and did not do it by choice. Their testimony was dishonest and non-accountable. Some were scared to admit their actual involvement, while others seemed scared of the repercussions outside of the courtroom if they spoke up, and then there was the group that had been too drunk or high to be accurate witnesses. It was hard to find a viable witness even though there had been over one hundred people at the party. Drunk and stoned people do not make reliable witnesses. It amazed when one seventeen year old girl testified at Eric's trial. She spoke of how she threw rocks at the roof because everyone else was. She was under the influence and she just joined in because everyone else was doing it. It painted a picture of how easy the mob mentality takes over. It also completely amazed me how many of the young people, some not even of legal age, that were called to be witnesses were not even escorted by their parents to court. I think that it is deplorable that a parent allow their child to attend court without support.

Throughout the entire court proceedings members of my family were always present. My brother was a constant and the rest of us would be there whenever we could. During sentencing all members of my immediate family prepared and presented their victim impact statements.

My oldest son, Matthew, presented his statement on the stand at times and other times I would read it for him. My daughter, Kaeleigh, would come to court every time there was sentencing and present her victim impact statement. She started this at the age of ten and was not finished until she was fourteen. My youngest son, Josh, would also come to court at times and I would read his statement for the court. I would present my husband's victim impact statement as well as my own.

My brother would present his victim impact statement to the court every time an assailant was up for sentencing. My sister in-law, Gail, filed hers with the courts to be read by the judge. My sister, Anneli, would also present her victim impact statement at time of sentencing. There would be times that I would have to present for her because in the four year period that the proceedings took place she was diagnosed with cancer and had to battle for her own life. My dad would also share his victim impact statement when he was able to be in court.

VICTIM IMPACT STATEMENT FROM ANITA LAMBERT
PLEASE DESCRIBE HOW THIS CRIME HAS AFFECTED YOU EMOTIONALLY

I don't even know where to begin on how to explain how this crime has affected me emotionally. I live every day of my life in heartbreak, fear and anger. The last thing I go to bed with and the first thing I awake to is the horrifying fact that I no longer have my nephew in my life. I have an emptiness inside of me. To have some you love ripped from you leaves scars that will never heal. My emotions are all over the place and I cannot ever really achieve happiness because of this cruel circumstance in my life. No longer is the bad news just on the television or in the newspaper. It is in my family and it has left me paralyzed emotionally. I have three children of my own and if I could put them in a bubble I would. Every day I fear for them at school and at play. I literally shake in fear when they are at the bus stop because I am scared someone will hurt them. As a mother it tears me up inside that my children have to experience firsthand the ugliness of this world. While other children are at the park playing and carefree my children have had to say goodbye to their cousin they love and then try to deal with all the emotions they are feeling. Do you know what it is like to be awakened constantly at night by a child screaming in fear for their life? I will tell you – It is sickening and heartbreaking and extremely emotionally taxing. I am angry that such evil could touch my family and that I am left with the fallout. Do you know what it is like to feel scared all the time? I live in fear because of other people's actions. I have had to climb out of a dark emotional hole so I could be a productive person again. I could not even go into a grocery store after Eric's death. It makes me so angry that my world has been completely and totally violated by the negative acts of others.

PLEASE DESCRIBE HOW THIS CRIME HAS AFFECTED YOU PHYSICALLY

Physically I am exhausted. I now have a sleeping disorder as well as I have had to overcome Post Traumatic Stress. Nightmares sap me of physical strength. Do you know what it is like to wake up nightly in a pool of sweat with your heart racing because of the nightmare you have had? The dreams of my nephew's death run over and over in my head. Some days it is hard for me to do my daily chores because of exhaustion. My high blood pressure has become a problem from all the stress that I am constantly dealing with. On top of that I have had other heart concerns all directly related to stress. Physically I also shake very bad and cannot control my tremors at times. All of these problems can be directly linked to this crime.

PLEASE DESCRIBE THE EFFECT THIS CRIME HAS HAD ON YOU LIFE

This crime has negatively impacted my life on so many levels. I am trying to deal with the effects of a violent crime with my children. At the time of the crime my children were: 12, 9, and 4. My oldest child did not want to leave the house and he became very angry, my middle child internalized everything and she lost her spunk in life, and my little one screamed in terror at night and was terrified that the bad boys that hurt Eric would come and get him. I have had to have counseling for some of my children. Crime has negatively touched them and they have lost their innocence. I also have lost my innocence. I was a fairly carefree and happy person and that has all changed. Do you know what it is like to hold someone you love and watch a machine register the pressure in their brain? You sit there for hours and hold them until their brain explodes and then collapses their brain stem and they die. That is what I relive daily. I think about how terrified Eric was before he was unconscious and it shatters my soul. Do you know what it is like to plead with your dying mother to live through her grandson's funeral because you need her to be strong for everyone? It breaks my heart that my mother had to die with such unhappiness, that she lost her grandson to such violence. Watching my brother and his family struggle to live daily with the loss of their son and brother is heart wrenching. Eric was a twin. My niece is missing a piece of herself that she will never get back. This crime has forever changed the path of my life. How dare the cruel acts of others ruin my life and my families!

VICTIM IMPACT STATEMENT FROM GRANT OLSEN (ERIC'S FATHER)

Emotional Affect

This process asks me to describe how this crime has affected me emotionally. Look around the room. Focus on someone that is here to support you, perhaps someone you love. Now imagine that chair being empty, forever.

The emotional impact immediately following the attack was like nothing I have ever experienced. I felt sick. Sitting in the hospital cafeteria on May 29, 2007 listening to the doctor tell me that Eric was not only not going to recover from his injuries, he was not going to survive was just the beginning of my nightmare.

The Doctor then went on to explain how the swelling in Eric's brain, caused by the attack, was going to force his brain out of his skull. It would be at this point that brain death would occur. When I asked the doctor how long until Eric would die, he couldn't tell me because, it was his opinion that Eric should not have survived as long as he had.

I spent 93 hours at the hospital waiting for my oldest son to die. I don't know if Eric heard me say that I loved him and that I would miss him. I don't know if he heard me talk to him about the dreams he had of completing his welding apprenticeship, about his girlfriend and how he thought she was a keeper, or about his desire to go on a trip somewhere warm in the winter.

I don't know if in his state of unconsciousness he could hear or understand anything of our final father son time together.

Once I got over my own initial anxiety, I had to leave Eric's bed and go share this news with family and friends. I was met with denial, anger and panic, no one would accept what I was telling them. I was forced into the position of being the strong one in this ordeal, I didn't want to be. Everybody else needed comfort, my family, Eric's friends. I saw all this pain and I couldn't fix it.

I felt helpless then and still do now. My wife still cries daily, and Eric's twin sister didn't show or embrace her grief for over a year, but when she finally did, it was intense. Both his sister and his 15 year old brother had the misfortune of watching Eric die before their eyes.

When the time came, even though it occurred exactly as the Doctor had explained, I was left with what was still the most difficult decision of my life. The decision to turn off Eric's life support. No parent should ever have to do that.

For a brief time, my grief turned to rage. My belief that the world was basically a good place was shattered. I wanted somebody to pay for this misery I was living immediately. I got past this and took steps both privately and in the media to discourage Eric's friends and supporters from retaliation. I am thankful that nothing serious came of the threats. No family deserves to go through this, yours included.

I still have trouble accepting that eight people, only one who I had ever seen before, are responsible for an attack that would lead to the death of my oldest son. It's been fifteen months, and I still don't know what all of Eric's attackers look like.

Physical Affect

While at the hospital waiting for Eric to die, I barely ate or slept. It took weeks before I could sleep through the night. I was tired and lacked energy to do, or focus on much of anything. Even after returning to work, it took effort just to get the basics done. These symptoms have subsided but return the night before each court date. Every time I come here, it is like this all happened yesterday. So far, it has been impossible for me to move on.

Effect on my Life

I still don't feel joy or sadness, or anything else at the level I did before Eric's death. I couldn't even shed a tear at my Mother's funeral in January of this year. I have little compassion for anyone anymore.

I have little interest in seeing or maintaining any kind of relationship with any of Eric's friends, some of whom were regular fixtures in our home for many years.

I am constantly concerned for the well-being of my son and daughter when they are out of my sight.

I look at any group of people on the street with suspicion. If I am approached by anyone, I take a defensive position.

The activities that my family and I used engage in for recreation aren't as appealing as they used to be. My wife and I barely socialize with anyone other than family. Holidays and Birthdays have turned in to days that I dread.

It has turned into a lonely existence for my wife and I.

This attack on Eric has ended his life, damaged his family, destroyed a romance and ended countless friendships.

Once you have completed whatever sentence this court hands out, your debt to society will be paid. Eric will still be dead, and all the collateral damage I just mentioned will remain. Think about this the next time you engage in an activity which may pose a serious risk to you or someone else.

It took four years to the day of the anniversary of Eric's death to complete all the legal aspects of his death. In the end not one sentence was just or long enough in my opinion. The sentencing was also upsetting to the Crown. The prosecutor in Colin Bibaud's trial considered an appeal. My brother, Grant, requested that this not be done. As a collective family group he felt that we could not endure the stress of court anymore.

At the end of all the court proceedings and trials I wrote this letter to Eric. I even published it on my blog. I knew that he would not be reading it. It was my way of starting to move forward. It may sound corny to some people but I referred to it often to push myself onward.

Dear Eric:

It is a rainy, windy, and cold day. It is like a parallel of my heart when you died. I look outside and it draws a picture of what my heart felt like when I walked away from you on that fateful night you left us – bleak and empty.

I wonder what would have become of you. Would you have been married by now, or travelled, or perhaps been a daddy? I will never know what could have been.

You are an inspiration to me. You have given me the tools to go out and make a difference and serve my human community. Without the tragedy of your death I would never have been equipped to serve in the capacity that I am. For this I can be thankful. I wish I never gained this experience but I must share it now that I have.

I remember what a little rascal you were. You were definitely a Neenee's boy. You would follow me around, sleep with me, tease me, and when you got older I think you attributed to my gray hair :) I love my memories of you and I will always hold them close to my heart. You were nothing if not UNIQUE!

Good Bye Eric! It is time for you to rest in Peace.

Love – Neenee

Part of my road to forgiveness is believing that these men must make restitution personally for their crimes or they will never have peace. Those without peace will never have a truly filled life. They will always have a shadow over them and in the end they will never live in any permanent happiness. They will have distorted relationships.

The fact that some of the men are living life in the shadow of divorce and estrangement from their families and have been rearrested and charged for other crimes leads me to believe that some of them have not taken the necessary steps to recover from the trauma of being a murderer. Anyone with a human sense of conscious will not be able to move forward until they have taken steps to make amends for what they have done.

You might be wondering what I think is necessary for them to do to attain peace. I don't think that they have to approach me or any member of my family to ask forgiveness. After my family presented our victim impact statements and before they were to be sentenced some of Eric's killers however did express their remorse and humility to us by saying they were sorry for their part in his death. The men that killed Eric must find it inside themselves to accept accountability and make a change in their hearts and actions to align their own true perspectives to live for the greater good. I believe as a Christian they must ask for forgiveness and accept Jesus in their hearts to truly achieve turning their lives around.

I want to be perfectly clear I am not some religious freak or fanatic. I am a believer. I believe we must all be accountable to God for our actions, accept responsibility for them, make amends for discourse, and strive to live a life that is not selfish but is selfless.

CHAPTER 9
SINKING

Death, despair, and despondency cloaked itself around me in darkness. It suffocated me, drawing me into a web of hatred, and became the very poisoned air I breathed. Every breath that I took filled me with more hazardous thoughts and feelings. Eventually I was under a mushroom cloud of evil, sinking deeper into a pit of nothingness. Eric was gone, my faith in the human race was gone, and my faith in God was being tested beyond any boundaries I could have ever imagined. Where was I to go from here?

Where I ended up going eventually was into a depression. Depression is one of those terms that sometimes brings to mind someone that stays in their pajamas all day, lies around, maybe has a blank stare, does not involve themselves with others, and cannot hold a conversation. This is the old school way of looking at depression. A lot of the time the person depressed hides it away from others so well that most people don't even know it is happening to their acquaintance, friend, or loved one.

Immediately after Eric died I did not go into the depression, I was in shock. My flight and fight instincts took over and I was on overload. I became very hypersensitive to being around people. I could not go into crowds like the grocery store and church, and picking my kids up from school put me in an absolute tizzy. I would be terrified at all times when my children were away from me that someone would steal them. I thought the worst of every situation and imagined evil lurking in every corner.

Fortunately I had my children to keep me going. I may have stayed in bed all day but they were young and needed me. I had to get up and face the day and force myself to keep life as normal as possible for them. I also could not take time to crash because I had a mom that needed care because she was dying of cancer and a dad that needed help dealing with the pressures put upon him. I had a brother and his family that were grieving the most horrendous death of a child and a sister and her family that were also grieving. My family needed me.

For months I just functioned on adrenalin overload.

My mom passed away January 31, 2008 and I started to fall. I was no longer running between her home an hour away and mine. But, I still was on a fight and flight plan. In the midst of all this I was running at least weekly (sometimes daily, or every other day) to court two and a half hours away. I never took time to settle and let my grief work itself out. I kept pushing it back down and it continued to fester and grow.

Many more months would pass and depression would start to seep into my soul. This was a depression born of hate and spite. It started to poison me.

I was a fairly good actor though, I could pull off looking fairly together for most people except those closest to me and even then I managed to hide the real raw emotion from them. My husband and children saw the signs of unhappiness. I was short tempered, I did not involve myself in things that would normally give me pleasure, and I lost my sense of humor. I think back now to times I would get so angry and blow things out of proportion. It usually involved a conflict in one of my children's activities or people in the service industry that were inefficient or rude. I had no patience for inept or unqualified people wasting my time because they didn't know what they were doing properly. With my family I wanted to protect them in bubble wrap so nothing would ever hurt them again.

There was one time in the summer after Eric passed away that I can remember my family and I were going to do yard work. Clarence wanted me to paint the trim on our shed while he made some other repairs. I am not sure what set me off but I became so distraught I locked myself in the bathroom, slid down the wall, and just sobbed. I could not stop crying and shaking. My family was pounding at the door to let them in but I would not unlock the door. It felt like my head was going to explode and I truly wanted to die. I did not want to keep living with the pain I was feeling all the time. Pushing down the pain allowed the pressure to build and it exploded that day. Matthew, my oldest son, picked the lock and came in and got me. He was only in grade seven. He should not have seen his mom in pieces like that. He managed to talk to me and get me calmed down enough and he took me outside to the rest of my family. Just being with them ended up giving me the feeling of wanting to live. It was a rare occasion that I showed my weak vulnerability. I usually covered my vulnerability up with angriness.

I became very sad, melancholy, and extremely impatient. Any little upset in my routine would cause me to stress out. Instead of talking in a normal voice I would shout, the smallest thing would upset me: like forgetting

Chapter 9

something on my shopping list. I had complete times of memory loss. Even to this day I meet people that I met during this time and I don't remember them. It has caused a few embarrassing situations when I ask who they are and they look at me like I am either crazy or rude. I've had periods of time that I just couldn't seem to fully remember. I suffered from nightmares that would leave me drenched in sweat and my chest so painful I could hardly breathe. These symptoms would happen on the rare occasion when I actually fell asleep. I would fixate on my own mortality and the mortality of my children. I would get tremors and the more anxious I became the more my body would shake. There were times when my body acted like I had Parkinson's disease and other times it would appear that I was having Grand Mal seizures.

Post-Traumatic Stress was the official title I received for how I felt. I went to a councillor in mental health at my local hospital on the request of my doctor. The councillor, though sympathetic, was not helpful at all. She did not have the proper training to deal with someone that was experiencing the type of complicated grief that I had. There are varying levels of grief which I did not realize. Grief due to murder is not equal in each situation. Someone who has lost a loved one to a quick shot in the head will have different grief than the person that slowly watches the life leave their loved one after being beaten. There are the imagines that come into a person's mind of the beating the loved one took, how the victim felt such terror until the time they became unconscious, the mental picture of crazed people standing over a loved one, the pain the victim felt while being attacked, blood and gore hits every recess of the mind. Sadly, with the special effects Hollywood can produce it gives someone the exact picture of what happens in a demented situation of the capacity of the pounding Eric endured. There were councillors in Edmonton, Alberta and Calgary, Alberta that were trained in complicated grief but these cities were two and a half hours away and I was not prepared to leave my family because I was already leaving them to go to court. Realistically it was just too much stress on me to have to leave my home another time.

Picking yourself up after a great lose is not an easy task. Everyone deals with grief in their own way. There is no "one cure fixes all" solution for grief. There are different types of grief. When my mom died it was a grief of sadness and loss but it was a "natural" event. So, while I mourned for my mom it was not a tormenting grief of senselessness. Eric's death created a grief of despair and despondency cloaking itself around me leaving me in darkness. It suffocated me, drawing me into a web of hatred, and became the very contaminated air I breathed. Every breath that I took filled me with more hazardous thoughts and feelings. A cloud of dissolution engulfed me. Making me sink deeper into a pit of nothingness.

Something had to change. I was living in a shell of a life. I had to address my depression, learn how to cope with my grief, address the post traumatic syndrome, and most of all forgive. As much as people wanted to help me I had to take these steps for myself. It is like anything in life if you want it you have to put the work into it. You also have to take time for grief. It cannot be rushed.

It took me about four years to get my grief for Eric to a manageable spot in my heart. In that time I would read books on grief, there were times when I would speak to my pastor about my grief. I have a very good friend that is a victim services provider and she gave me reading resources to help me navigate my pain. I did not go to any other grief counselling or support groups because I felt out of place. My grief was created from a heinous act and I did not want to tell my story to people that were suffering themselves and were not equipped to deal with the gory facts of my grief. Until I lived this madness I know that I would be uncomfortable and horrified if someone came to me with the same circumstance I was forced to live with.

I mostly depended on myself to control my grief. I would box it away and not acknowledge it. The sad thing about doing that though is that your emotions build up and over time explode. I would be living my life and all of a sudden something as simple as seeing a picture of Eric would trigger an overwhelming sadness in me and my grief would be raw and piercing again.

The old adage, "time heals" is true. Time did help me with my grief to a point. My true breakthrough in my grief happened though with forgiveness. It wasn't until I moved passed my feelings of hate and wanting restitution that I was able to truly manage my grief.

Even to this day I grieve. You never get over grief. It makes me furious when people make comments like: It's time to get over your grief or haven't you dealt with your grief yet? You never get over a loved one dying, you learn to manage it. I grieved for what Eric was to me, what he was to his family, and what he could have been one day. He had his whole life to develop character, become a husband, a father, or whatever he wanted and it was ripped away. It is okay to grieve in a positive way as long as you are not consumed by your grief. It is true that to grieve deeply means you have loved completely. I believe this with all my heart and I know there will always be a sadness in me that I have lost Eric and that he is not here on this Earth with me to love.

Instead of grieving with hate in my heart I now channel that energy to improving a little piece of the world today. I use my grief to talk to youth about their feelings, habits, and lifestyles. I try to provide a positive role model for them by teaching them through example that feelings of hatred and retribution don't bring happiness and definitely don't bring back a loved one. It just destroys your own life in the process.

CHAPTER 10
CHOICE

Choice is truly one of the most important tasks a person can exercise. There are those in our world that cannot choose external forces in their lives like: where they live, if they live in external danger or peace, how they provide for themselves or their families, they cannot choose the actions of others or how those actions play out in their lives, they cannot always control their health or how their body reacts to certain ailments and disease. It is however possible for everyone to use their exercise of choice on how they internally choose to deal with these external forces. This is a huge life lesson that I had to learn.

When you have experienced a travesty such as the murder of a loved one it is easy to fall and not pick yourself up and regain your life. There is no doubt that you have earned the right to wallow in your grief. It is however time sensitive! You cannot wallow forever or you are truly not living.

There is no ten step process for forgiveness, for moving forward, or for regaining composure. Each individual is different and everyone has their own process for healing. My process is unique to me but it was built on a foundation of Christian belief, life experience, and interaction with others. There is however one common point in the process of healing that everyone shares – CHOICE!

The first step in the process of truly living again after tragedy is choice. No one can force you to get up in the morning, laugh, live, or move forward. You need to truly want to regain your life back. Sometimes people feel they are only accountable to themselves. If they choose to let life leach from them it will not affect anyone. That is such a narrow minded attitude. Even if you do not have children, like I did, depending on you to provide the necessities of day to day life for them there is always someone or something you need to be accountable to. For me God expects and demands more than self-centeredness. If you choose to live in a life of darkness you are not living the principles of humanity.

I never knew how profound the power of choice was until I had to make choices for myself to start truly living life again. It is so easy to let life's events take over and pull you under. It takes strength of will and character to fight against it. It takes a conscious effort to rise above negativity. I do believe though that everyone has the potential to do this if they choose, but it takes daily work and it is by no means easy.

There are times too that you need to accept the help of others. Doing this is also scary. It means you are not controlling everything in your realm. You are choosing to let someone else influence you. I was a very self-sufficient person. I had to accept humility and allow others to support me. I could not do it on my own anymore. I had to choose to accept help and actively seek help from others.

My husband, Clarence, was the first one to really bridge my self-centeredness and gain access to how I was truly feeling. It was not an easy day when my husband told me that I was no longer good for our children, for him, and most importantly for myself. I took a real hit to my pride that day along with every other feeling that was going on inside of me. I thought I had hidden my true feelings from everyone. My behavior though was telling a different tale.

Even though I did not rage or physically lash out at my children, me negatively commenting and getting upset with every other driver on the road or a lazy waitress or the hundreds of other inept people that I would meet in a day was not influencing them in a positive manner. I tended to raise my voice more than I ever had before. My comedian side had left and all that it was replaced with was a morose and serious person with no humor in her eyes or soul anymore. I did not spend time building beautiful crafts, sharing meaningful moments, or really giving of myself. I would play games, read books, go for bike rides and walk, but I would not be with my kids in spirit. I was just going through the motions. I was detached and my family needed me to reattach myself. In a fast moment of time they lost their cousin and their mom. It wasn't fair.

Six months after my mom passed away my husband, children, father, and I headed off to Yellowstone Park, USA for a long talked about holiday. This was a holiday that my mom was always supposed to be a part of. We camped next to an older couple in Idaho for a week. In that weeks' time my daughter, Kaeleigh, and the woman next door, Lolly, became soulmates. I really believe God created this scenario for them to meet. Kaeleigh was devastated from losing my mom, her nana. Lolly had never had a little girl and she was a great distance away from her own grandchildren. It was God directing kindred spirits to one another. Lolly and her husband, Bud, had two dogs. Kaeleigh wandered over and asked if she could pet the dogs and from that moment on a friendship bloomed. They formed the most remarkable bond between two strangers. Lolly lived in Phoenix, Arizona and after a week together both Kaeleigh and her felt like they were losing their best friend as we pulled away from the campground one morning on our way home. Kaeleigh and Lolly would continue their friendship for the next six months via email and snail mail with the odd phone call thrown in.

In February Clarence contacted Lolly and asked her if she would like Kaeleigh and I to come and visit her. She was elated. Now you have to realize how out of character this was for Clarence to contact someone he had only met for a week in the summer. Clarence knew that something had to change and he left his comfort zone to help make this happen. He surprised Kaeleigh and I with a trip to Arizona to meet up with Lolly and her husband, Bud. During this time he wanted me to rest, rejuvenate, and regain my composure. I promised him that when I came home I would have a plan on how to get myself back on track.

That week was a God send. I was given the chance to leave my day to day tasks and stresses behind, I could rest, I only had to think about myself and my daughter, I was not faced with court or with the prying eyes and opinions of people around me. It was very frustrating having parts of your life displayed on television or in the newspaper. I had to deal with people grilling my two oldest children for details of their cousin's murder. At one point the Vice-Principal of my daughter's school had to have a talk with her teacher because he would ask her questions about it in class. She was in grade three. I was so appalled that someone would do that to a child. There was also the continuous chatter and speculation of people that knew me and everyone had an opinion. I was actually told by a member of my congregation at Church who came to visit me at home (even though I had requested no visitors except my Pastor) that it was probably better off this happened to Eric because he was living a sinful life and deserved what he got. Words cannot even explain how upset I was by this "well meaning" Christian. My pastor was so good. He told me to take pity on them that they could be that insensitive and stupid. I had an extended member of my family tell me it was for the best Eric died before he did something equally as bad. These comments hit me right down to my soul. I knew that Eric was not an innocent bystander but no one deserved to die in the manner he did. I loved him and even though he behaved badly in some situations that love did not lessen.

In Phoenix I had time to think and pray, and God also provided me with wonderful friends, Lolly and Bud. Lolly and Bud are an integral part of my family today. They spend holidays with my family and I, we visit them regularly, we chat on the phone regularly, and my entire family has welcomed them as family.

Lolly, is to say the least, a very wise woman. She is very educated and sound in her theology, she is insightful on all topics of concern, and she has keen listening skills. I dare say she is a great mentor. God placed this wonderful woman in my life to help me in my struggles. She has provided support, advice, and if I have needed it criticism. Lolly taught me lessons on forgiveness. She would pray with me and for me.

My trip to Arizona was the beginning of reclaiming the choices I had made up until that point. Initially when Eric was killed I went into a fight or flight mode with my emotions, cutting myself off from everyone and everything except my family and closest friends, that would not let me push them away. Later after my mom passed away I crashed and became depressed. This depression did not show it's self in its stereotypical form of languish and sadness. It hid itself behind anger and hate. Hate so engrained that it poisoned many of my relationships, life experiences, and how I dealt with people out of my family realm. I was always looking for the negative in every action that someone did, it was almost like a conspirator theory – everyone was out to hurt me our mine.

One of the decisions I came to on that trip was to book an appointment with my doctor and talk to him about anti-depressants. Yes, I was going to admit to someone that I was not right in the head. My night terrors had to be addressed and the post traumatic had to be acknowledged. I had to convince myself that it was okay to say the "mentally ill" words. There is such a stigma concerning mental illness, even in todays' society. I did not want people to think of me as a nutcase. I also did not want to be weak. Strong people don't need help.

I have since learned that it takes a strong person to admit they need help. To make the choice to admit that you are not well and need professional help is not easy. At least for me it wasn't easy.

After coming home I made an appointment with my doctor. Making the choice to take antidepressants became a lot easier for me once my doctor explained the actual physiological effects of stress and depression. If you do not address stress and depression it can actually change your brain makeup. By taking the medication I could control the chemistry in my brain so that I did not suffer irreparable damage. I never realized that being so "sad" could create psychological disease and permanent damage.

I was prescribed sleeping pills that would literally knock me out. I did not use them very often but when I did I could sleep without terror waking me up throughout the night. When you go for long periods of time without sleep it compounds the anxiety and tension a person deals with. The human body is not as able to fight off sickness, regain strength, or handle situations properly with lack of sleep. Recovering from Post-Traumatic Stress took medication it was not simply mind over matter.

After starting the anti-depressant medication I became much more leveled in my emotions and would not be so irrational in my thinking that there was always something or someone out to get me or the ones I loved. It was a very positive choice that I made to follow through with my doctor. Taking medication was only one of the many choices I had to make on my road of healing. Looking back now it was probably by far the easiest one to stick to.

CHAPTER 11
LOOKING THROUGH THE EYES
OF GRACE

When someone hates like I did for so long it becomes part of their daily routine. It is like waking up in the morning and putting on a pair of glasses that you wear throughout the day that actually distorts the reality of situations so much that you see life in grays and black not in an array of colors.

The power of choice has been the common theme throughout my healing process. It comes with a price but like anything you get what you pay for. I had to keep moving forward and by far the hardest hurdle for me to overcome was the hatred that burned within me. I was not going to learn to manage my grief until I had dealt with the anger and destructive thoughts I had towards Colin, Cody, Darwin, Daniel, Charles, Tristan, Danny, and Joel. Without forgiveness there is not peace.

Once I made the decision that living with hatred or

never ending despair was not the choice I wanted for myself I was on the road to healing. My road took lots and lots of prayer. At times when I was driving two and a half hours to court I would literally be talking out loud to God saying things like, "Please let me stay calm." Or," God please help me not to rip someone's faceoff." I had to choose to depend on my faith and beliefs to help me through the bad stuff.

I believe prayer led to the other steps of healing for me. God placed people, situations and thoughts in my path to strengthen me and guide me. Again though I had to choose to follow through with nudges God gave me. I had to choose to accept them.

One day my pastor, Dale Hansen, told me about a book he would like me to read. He knew the struggles I was having. I believe God placed this book in his hands so he could pass it along to me. The story was called "Left to Tell: Discovering God Amidst the Rwandan Holocaust" by Immacule'e Ilibagiza. I trusted my Pastor as he was also a very good friend to my family and me so I choose to read the book. I could have just as easily put it down and never opened it up but I wanted to respect my friend so I read it.

It was the most remarkable story of forgiveness I had ever heard. It told the story of a young woman's plight from Rwanda and how she was able to attain forgiveness for those that destroyed her home, brutally murdered her family, and completely altered her life. She found the grace to forgive her enemies.

I could not imagine the spirit of this woman to forgive those that had literally raped and murdered her family and displaced her. How does someone achieve that level of forgiveness? And, why would you bother? I thought the best thing that would happen was the men that killed Eric would be gang beaten themselves or worse, maybe then they would realize what they had done.

Immacule'e Ilibagiza was a woman of God. She lived her life as a Christian and as a Christian she knew that in order to please God she had to choose to forgive. God gives us grace and strength in the face of enormous adversity. I had yet to fully realize that in order for me to be right in my mind and heart I had to be right with God. It was going to take forgiveness in order for me to start living in the light He had prepared for me.

I had to honestly admit to myself that I had not truly forgiven and that I needed to completely give this hatred to God to deal with. Once I achieved this step, I began to find my true road to healing. I can honestly say that making that move saved my sanity, my health, and my family. It was also complete proof that God is active in our lives if we let Him. I know without a doubt that I could not have gained this level of forgiveness without His help.

I do not shy away from letting anyone know my personal belief system. I believe that with God all things are possible. I am a Christian and I also believe that it is my responsibility to forgive, to live a life within boundaries of decency, and contribute to society in a positive manner. These are principles of humanity.

No matter what God means to you or whatever that represents to you in your belief system the principles of humanity are the same for every earthly citizen. You are required to make the most out of your life here on Earth in the most positive way. Why else would we exist?

I chose to attend bible study at my church on Thursday mornings. This was another nudge from God I believe. I was the spring chicken in the crowd. I was literally thirty years younger than everyone else. These mornings provided great guidance to me. My spiritual mentor, Dorothy Bolton, was another gift angel from God. She has prayed for me, cried for me, guided me, and supported me throughout my tribulations. One of the greatest things Dorothy has taught me is: HATE THE SIN NOT THE SINNER. It sounds so simplistic but if a person can step back and see that it is the actions that someone does that is hateful and hurtful it is easier to cope with a situation.

Learning this simplistic truth took some time. It was not an automatic turnaround for me. I think that God was placing people and situations in my path to help me regain my spirit and life. Even certain songs on the radio would make me sit up and take notice. There is one song in particular that really stood out in my mind with a message. It was "Forgiveness" by Matthew West. One portion of the lyrics says, "Even when the jury and the judge, Say you gotta right to hold a grudge, It's the whisper in your ear saying 'Set It Free'." This line resonated the Crown Prosecutor's want to appeal sentencing for some of the perpetrators. The other portion of the song that really stood out for me on how I felt was, "It'll clear the bitterness away, It can even set a prisoner free, There is no end to what it's power can do, So, let it go and be amazed, By what you see through eyes of grace, The prisoner that it really frees is you."

Pastor Dale and I talked about forgiveness. He understood that my devastation was not merely a small slight it was a huge offense. I had in my thought process that in order to really forgive these men I had to talk to them and embrace them as fellow human beings. I thought they were monsters! I was not about to embrace a monster.

Pastor Dale explained the concept of spiritual

forgiveness to me. Forgiveness is not merely an act. There was no expectation on me to physically embrace the men that killed Eric. I was not expected to meet with them face to face, exchange Christmas cards, or have any actual physical contact with the defendants. Forgiveness is a belief or mind set. It is allowing you the freedom to live in joy and happiness without the bulk of negativity. It is giving over the judgement to God so that you can be free. It empowers you and discredits your adversary. They can no longer hold power over you. You are free. When I was allowing hatred to eat up my soul and make me act out negatively, not interact with those I loved properly, and generally not enjoy life, the men that killed Eric were killing me slowly too. I had to choose to set myself free from that pain.

Learning to forgive is not the same as actually forgiving. You can say the words and know it is the right thing to do but unless you actually make the change from hate to forgiveness you do not reap the personal benefits. There were many times over the years after Eric's death that I would hugely struggle with forgiveness. To this day there are times when I have to beat down the hatred and remember that it is in God's hands. Matthew 6:14-15 says, "for if you forgive other people when they sin against you, your heavenly Father will also forgive you.

But if you do not forgive others their sins, your Father will not forgive your sins."

I know that having my Christian Faith is truly the reason I have pulled through the darkness and into the light. God placed numerous people in my path to help me along the way. Some of these people physically showed me the grace of God, some of them openly prayed for me, some were sounding boards when I was struggling, some provided unconditional love even when I was not the most loveable, and others prayed for me behind the scenes. I have heard from people throughout the last nine years how they prayed for me. They prayed for happiness, peace, and for my will to turn to God's will not my own.

I would pray and sometimes feel like He was not listening. I would pray for happiness and a way to live a more light filled life. All along I needed to pray for strength to forgive. Forgiveness can free you from dragging the sorrow of hate and permitting the trauma to crumble your times of happiness. Once I was able to forgive my life started to come together.

CHAPTER 12
THE PHYSICALITIES OF STRESS

Not only does constantly being "sad" have psychological effects on a person, it can also have physical affects. Compound sadness with stress, grief, and hate it can create very serious physical debilitation. Some of the physical manifestations cannot be altered or improved once a person has dealt with all the negativity and started living in a positive fashion again. Negativity has profound effects on the human body that can be crippling.

Lack of sleep and extreme stress can lead to auto immune disease. Being on a flight and fight mode for so many years left me vulnerable to physical illness. Illness that I will have to live with for the rest of my life. I wish that I could have sped up my healing process. Perhaps if I had acknowledge my hate, faced it, and forgiven sooner I would not have irreparably damaged myself. Please think of this if you are facing the same feelings I had.

For the past six years I have complained that

everything in my body hurts. So many doctors treated me as if I was neurotic or depressed. I seriously cannot stand the feel of many materials on my skin, there are times when even the slightest touch feels like someone has beat me, or hitting a pothole in the car can feel like I have been dropped from a ten storey building. I am super sensitive to noise and at times cannot even handle the sound of my kids' music playing or being in a group of people talking. I forget things and when I am really suffering I completely lose my train of thought. Two years ago I was finally referred to a doctor that specialized in pain. He diagnosed me with fibromyalgia. Fibromyalgia is an extremely misunderstood chronic pain disease that is just now being recognized in the medical community.

It was so liberating to finally have someone take me seriously on how I was feeling. I knew I wasn't depressed because I had totally experienced depression earlier on and this was not at all the same thing. It was truly physical and it was debilitating. There were times when I was hardly out of bed for the day except to do what I had to for my family because I hurt so badly.

When my specialist made my diagnosis I felt a sense of relief. Someone actually listened to me. I was on the road to gaining my physical life back.

I had to have a very in-depth patient history taken.

My specialist wanted to know every aspect of my life from medical to emotional. When we got to the time in my life when Eric was killed he took copious amounts of notes. He made me explain in detail how I handled or did not handle the stress of Eric's murder. He said without doubt the trauma of losing Eric and living in a flight and fight mode for so long completely wore down my physical system. Then to add insult to my system I held on to such hatred for so long that it took its toll as well. There is actual science to stress overload and hormones and chemicals in the body that can lead to disease. I am not going to delve into that because frankly I am not a doctor and it makes no difference to me. What I am centred on is the trauma that Eric's killers placed on me and the fact that my own lack of self-care and healing led to my demise.

My pain control requires work. There are five aspects that I must follow in order to stay healthy and productive. I must address the medical side of my life (taking pain control medicines), my physical self (I must exercise daily and eat good foods), my spiritual life (I must honor my beliefs and live accordingly), my mental health (this is how I deal with the day to day stresses I live with) and also my emotional self (how much baggage I have). It amazed me when my doctor laid out my pain control regime for me that it circled back to getting rid of stress and hatred and being true to my personal belief system. These were the same concepts I had to address to gain my emotional health back after Eric was killed. The concepts that I have explained in the earlier chapters.

My fibromyalgia is controllable most days. There are definite things that can create me to go into a flare: weather, altitude, sickness, some food additives such as aspartame, and worst of all STRESS! If I do no deal with my stress and allow things to eat at me in quick time I will be sick and it will take anywhere from a day to a week for me to gain back my physical health.

I have learned over time certain tools that help with this: walking my dog, quiet time spent with my family, yoga, prayer, journaling, and rest. When I have a flare I continue my work in honoring Eric and it makes me feel better on the inside, even though my physical self might not be stellar. There are times that presenting my story actually brings on a flare because of the stress of reliving every detail of Eric's death over again. Writing this book has had its own hurdles to conquer, especially in the early chapters when I laid out the circumstances of Eric's beating. That's okay though because I am working towards a greater good, teaching forgiveness, encouraging positive choices, and making a change. To me that is a positive stress that I will happily deal with.

Taking control of your emotions and ridding yourself from hate does not just bring healing to your mental self it allows your physical self to recuperate from trauma to its system as well. You owe it to yourself to make positive choices that will reflect positivity in your overall body health. Choose to prioritize what is more important – self-love vs. hateful spite. It doesn't sound like a tough decision when you say it out loud but in practice it is one of the hardest decisions of your life.

CHAPTER 13
SUCCESS WITH A CHANGE OF HEART

On November 25, 2009 I honored my promise to Eric to try and make a difference in the world. It was baby steps but I started a web blog with the help of my two oldest children. I first started the idea thinking that it was basically going to be a rant page about the injustices of the world. The more I talked about it with my kids and started to think about it the more the idea developed into taking on a perspective of positive change. The blog is www.wwwvoice-of-reason.com. Under the title on the blog it reads: Eric is my reason and I am using my voice to stop the violence!

I started writing articles for the blog that would address everyday problems, promote positive growth, enhance social awareness, and on some level fight against corruption and stupidity. The blog grew into another step. I started presenting and sharing the story of Eric's death and how it affected me throughout Central Alberta. I developed a classroom program where I would go in and share all the dirt and chaos that murder entails. It was my hope that by the very graphic and honest nature of my presentations teens would realize the devastation that can ensue when you combine drugs, alcohol, violence, and hatred.

Beaten to a coma, he died as she watched

Rocky's Anita Lambert watched her nephew
Eric Olson die after 2007 gang beating

Eric Olsen, 20, was attacked by a mob of drunken, stoned youth who beat him unconscious and then put him in a coma from which he never recovered.

Anita Lambert told the story of her nephew's murder by a group of 22 to 25 people May 27, 2007 near Stony Plain.

The early years of my presentations were very focussed on the hurt and devastation that was left behind after Eric was killed. I was very honest about my emotions and how it destroyed my life. I was never vengeful in my presentations for two reasons. First, I would not be allowed the honor of working with youth if I was not composed and positive. Secondly, I was starting to fool myself that I had forgiven the men that had done this to Eric and my family.

Once I had changed my heart to actual forgiveness my presentations focussed on the positivity of choice. I used my voice to encourage young people to be positive in their life stories. One of the hardest times in someone's life is the adolescent and teenage years. These are very formative years for developing character. It is absolutely necessary to give youth examples and tools to develop proper positive choice protocol.

Presenting to youth and gaining their feedback and perspective was very gratifying to me. It still is. I was making a positive impact on the lives of others. I had students talk to me about their lives and experiences and how listening to me speak helped them. I had one young girl talk to me about her addiction and how telling my story made her realize how she was hurting herself and her family. I had a young man that constantly used violence when he was upset. He had not fully grasp that in an instant violence could perpetuate to death until he listened to me. He did not want something like that on his conscious. Another young lady was the victim of incest. She was molested by her father. She was estranged from him but had so much hate and anger burning within her. I couldn't blame her, being hurt by the one person who should protect you the most was the ultimate betrayal. She was self-medicating with drugs and alcohol to rid herself of the memories, lashing out at authority, and other times withdrawing completely within herself. This young lady stayed in the classroom after the rest of her classmates left to talk to me. She told me her heartbreaking story. When she was done she said she was going to try and forgive him so she could move on with her life. She had never understood that forgiving did not mean that she had to see him and actually talk and tell him that he was forgiven. It was rewarding to make a difference.

My mantra was: If I could make a difference in one person's life I had achieved what I set out to do. I still live by this. I have been honored by the words and thoughts that youth have shared with me. Their openness showed me that I am truly making a positive difference in the lives of young people.

"No matter what you do you never deserve to be killed. I think those kids had no right in what they did. And, it tells me that I need to make sure that I make the right choices at parties. I don't ever want to put my family in a spot like that or have anything happen to my brother no matter what he does. I'll be there to keep him safe."

~Brandon (Student)

"I went to a party after a baseball tournament. I started drinking with friends. I've done something stupid. I was judged for it. I haven't been able to live it down since. Hearing about this story made me feel sad. I've learnt that alcohol and drugs have a huge factor on peoples' decisions. Everyone's mistakes are based on it. I grew up around drugs. My 3 brothers smoke pot. I've seen things. I've never tried and never want to now."

~Unknown (Student)

"Thank you so much for coming into our class and sharing your story. You have turned a story of tragedy into a powerful message of forgiveness and compassion I was so touched by your words and it forced me to examine my own relationships. Thank you so much for your insight, honesty, and courage.

'Unless someone like you cares a whole awful lot, nothing is going to get better. It's not!' Dr. Seuss"

~Miranda (Teacher)

CHAPTER 14
SOCIAL ACCOUNTABILITY

Dealing with Eric's death has brought me a sense of social responsibility. I am compelled now to actively make the world a better place. I was always good at volunteering for my children's activities or helping out in their classrooms. I feel bound now to make use of my resources in a broader spectrum to develop awareness, support for the vulnerable, and even aide in the understanding bureaucracies have of victims of homicide and what they need for support. These endeavours also help me in the healing process because they are focussed on my mantra: If I can make a difference in one person's life I had achieved what I set out to do.

I am currently the Vice Chair and Secretary for The Rocky and District Victim Services Unit board. The Unit is a non-profit organization that's focus is to: Encourage Victims to Move Forward! The Unit provides resources and support for victims of crime and crisis.

I have shared my story at various conferences. I am actively seeking to expand upon my classroom presentations as well as presenting to other organizations and groups including: juvenile prisoners, youth groups, victim services conferences, and social awareness gatherings.

My home is an open door to youth that want to make a change in their lives. My family and I have helped with those that have made the choice to stop taking drugs and need to have a safe nonjudgmental place for a while. Some come just for a meal, others for a couple days, and some have stayed a few months.

I know that God is not done with me yet. He still has areas of work for me to explore. I need to stay open to making a change in the world.

God continues to put people in my path that influence me in a positive direction. The idea for this book came from my sister-in-law, Maxine, she knew of an author with a similar story. Maxine encouraged me to read her story and from it I gained inspiration.

I have been trying for a few years to get my story written but kept coming up with excuses of why it wasn't getting done: I didn't know where to start, my kids are too young for me to focus on writing and not them, I am too busy…Then on July 25, 2015 I was the mistress of ceremonies for Theo Fleury's Victorwalk. After he shared his story that day I talked to him about Eric's death and my road to forgiveness. He encouraged me to contact his publisher to share my story. I filed away the idea in the back of my mind. In August of that same summer I contacted Julie Salisbury, of Influence Publishing. She encouraged me to enroll in her writing seminar and publishing program that started September 2015. All of this led to where I am at today.

With my own power of choice, support from those around me, and God's enlightening Spirit I have been able to discard my cloak of darkness, hatred, and pain. I have stepped into the light. I have choose not to go backwards into the dark but push forward through the light. Shade will sometimes shadow me, but through choice and God's strength I have been able to continue my journey.

My journey did not begin in an instant. It has been a gradual progression from warm up to endurance and I believe it is a journey that will never end. Choices will have to be made and discarded or changed. Pathways will be altered. Roadblocks will appear and have to be conquered. Not all my choices will be the right ones but it is my hope that I will learn from them and move forward.

Right now I am on an uncharted course that I am just discovering. I am discovering my own human elements. And, one of the most important elements that I have been gifted with is the power of choice. I cannot control all what happens to me. I can however control or choose how I deal with what is presented to me. The only person I can control in life is myself. I have chosen my actions to exude positive power and influence.

Author Biography

 Anita resides just on the edge of the very peaceful and engaging Rocky Mountains. She is a stay at home mother of three children, wife, aunt, daughter, sister, and friend. Anita is very rooted in family values and caring for those she loves. May 31, 2007 drastically changed her life forever. She has lived through devastation that ensues after a love one is murdered. With her personal insight, she has moved forward providing advocacy for victims, a voice to youth through raw presentation of her story, and fundraising for the Rocky and District Victim Services Unit non – profit organization.

CPSIA information can be obtained
at www.ICGtesting.com
Printed in the USA
LVOW10s0539260117
522114LV00003B/16/P